JANE GOODALL'S ANIMAL WORLD

ELEPHANTS

by Miriam Schlein

Scientific Consultant: Cynthia Moss
Photographs by Leonard Lee Rue III and Len Rue, Jr.

A Byron Preiss Book

ALADDIN BOOKS
MACMILLAN PUBLISHING COMPANY   NEW YORK
COLLIER MACMILLAN PUBLISHERS   LONDON

◇ Introduction: The Elephant by Jane Goodall

When I first arrived in Africa, I wanted to study elephants. They are such majestic animals, so amazingly intelligent. They have such wonderful relationships with each other.

The first time I ever saw elephants in the wild was in the forests near the Ngorongoro Crater, in Tanzania. I was with the park warden. We had heard the trumpeting call of an angry elephant, and the warden had let me follow him through the trees to find out what was going on.

They were about fifty yards away when we saw them. Two young bull elephants were having a quarrel, and one was being chased around a clump of bushes. Suddenly he turned and stood his ground. His rival, ears out and trunk in the air, trumpeted and charged. There was a clash of tusks and the smaller elephant ran off.

The trumpeting call of the elephant is, for me, the most exciting sound of the African bush. And it can be terrifying too. Once when my husband and I were out in the bush, a whole herd gathered, angry at our intrusion. First one and then another of the enraged cows raised her trunk and trumpeted, ears outstretched. Suddenly one led the charge toward us. Fortunately, she was bluffing—just before she reached our Landrover she stopped and wheeled away. The other stopped, too, and they all moved off. My husband and I were left with trembling knees!

It is only in places where elephants are hunted that they become so aggressive. And today they are snared, chased, and killed for their ivory almost everywhere in Africa. Anyone who has watched a film of an elephant slaughter will understand why they fear and hate us.

In all the years I have been in Africa, one of the most wonderful moments was when Iain Douglas-Hamilton took me to meet some of the elephants he and his wife had studied for so many years in Tanzania's Lake Manyara National Park. After about two hours, we finally met Virgo, Iain's special elephant friend. We got out of the car and walked toward her, and she left her herd and came to meet us. And then, as I stood beside Iain, Virgo, a wild African elephant, reached out her trunk and touched my outstretched hand. Somehow, together, we must reach out to help the last remaining elephants in the wild.

◇ Contents

◇ Where Do Elephants Live?

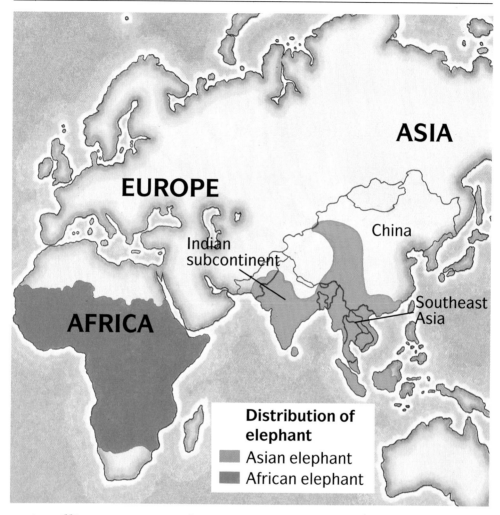

A million years ago, there were elephants in North America, South America, Europe, Asia, and Africa. Now elephants are found only in Africa and Asia.

African elephants live in Africa south of the Sahara Desert, except at the southern tip of South Africa.

Asiatic elephants (usually called "Indian elephants") are found throughout the Indian subcontinent in India, Bhutan, Bangladesh, and Nepal; throughout Southeast Asia in Thailand, Malaysia, Laos, Vietnam, Kampuchia (formerly called

Cambodia), the island of Sri Lanka (formerly called Ceylon), and Myanmar (formerly called Burma); and in the Yunan province of southern China.

Elephants are adaptable animals. They can survive in different kinds of habitats. Some live on grassy lands called *savannahs*. Some live deep in rain forests. Some inhabit dry areas, and some roam mountain areas more than 10,000 feet above sea level.

A work elephant crosses a river in Asia.

African elephants on a plain in Kenya, Africa. Mount Kilimanjaro rises in the background.

◇ The Family Tree of the Elephant

Elephants belong to the order or group of animals called *Proboscidea* (pruh-bah-*sid*-ee-uh). The name comes from the word "proboscis," meaning "long snout or nose." The earliest proboscideans we know of lived forty or fifty million years ago. One was called *Moeritherium* (mer-uh-*theer*-ee-yum) and looked more like a pig than an elephant. It stood about three feet high, lived in swamps, and had no trunk at all. Other early proboscideans were *Phiomia* (fee-*o*-me-uh) and *Paleomastodon*. These were bigger, and Paleomastodon did have a small trunk. All three lived in Africa.

Many different proboscideans developed and spread throughout the world. Among these were "hoe-tuskers" that had tusks shaped like a hoe, and "shovel-tuskers," whose long lower jaws and tusks were flat, like a shovel. Scientists think

African elephant

Asian elephant

6

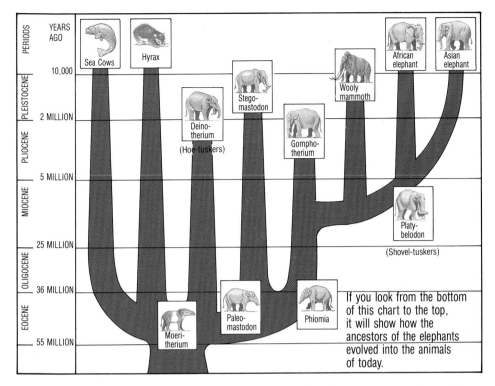

If you look from the bottom of this chart to the top, it will show how the ancestors of the elephants evolved into the animals of today.

the elephant's trunk developed from the long upper lip above the "shovel-tusk."

There have been about 350 different species of elephants that we know of. Now there remain just two species: the African elephant (*Loxodonta africana*) and the Asiatic or Indian elephant (*Elephas maximas*). The African elephant is larger, with bigger ears. At the end of its trunk it has two "fingers"; the Asiatic elephant has one. There is also a small African forest elephant that is about seven feet high (*Loxodonta africana cyclotis*).

The animals that are most closely related to the elephant today are the little furry hyrax and the sea mammals known as "sea cows"—the dugong and the manatee. The tooth and leg structure of the hyrax and elephant are similar, as are the teeth of the elephant and the sea cows. Hyraxes, sea cows, and elephants probably all share some common ancestor that lived more than fifty million years ago.

◇ The Elephant Community

Female elephants, called cows, live in family groups. Usually the leader is the oldest female. The family group consists of the leader and her daughters, along with other females and their calves. The usual size of the group is eleven or twelve, though the number can be as high as twenty-four elephants or as few as two or three.

Family groups often feed and move around with certain other family groups. Sometimes they part for a few days, but sooner or later they join up again. These larger groupings are called "kin" or "bond" groups, because scientists think they may be related to one another.

Family groups usually stay together as a family, though sometimes an adult female may leave to form her own group. A big herd of elephants is generally made up of a number of family groups, all moving together.

Around the age of fourteen, the young males leave their

family group and join a group of adult males, or bulls. From then on, they spend most of their time with this all-male group.

Bulls lead a different kind of life. A herd of bulls, usually numbering twenty or thirty but sometimes well over 100, may stay together for a while, eating, drinking, and traveling with each other for a few days or weeks. But the bulls don't have the stable and long-lasting connections the female elephants have with one another. They frequently shift from one herd to another.

Adult bulls usually travel with a female group only when one of the cows is in *estrus*—ready to mate. The bulls stay for a few days, mate, then join up with the herd of bulls again.

Bulls twenty-five years old or older may periodically show a condition called *musth*, during which time they are very eager to mate. Bulls will fight each other for the right to mate. Otherwise there is not much fighting between elephants.

Among the bulls, as with the females, the leader, or dominant one, is usually the oldest and strongest.

◇ Sizing Up the Elephant

The African elephant is the largest land mammal living today. The Asiatic elephant is the second largest, and the white rhino of Africa is the third. All of these land giants are dwarfed by the largest mammal of all—the 100-foot-long blue whale.

Some elephants of the past were even larger than today's elephants. *Paleoloxodon* (pale-ee-oh-*lox*-uh-don), a now extinct species that lived in Europe and Africa five million years ago, probably reached a height of fourteen feet. And some were smaller. Dwarf elephants of Malta were only three feet high.

Unlike most mammals, elephants keep growing for most of their lives. So the oldest are generally the largest. Males are much larger than females of the same age.

Measurement:
height at shoulders

African elephant
7-13 feet

Indian elephant
9-11 feet

White rhinoceros
5-6½ feet

Hippo
4½-5⅓ feet

Pygmy hippo
2½-3 feet

◇ How the Elephant Moves

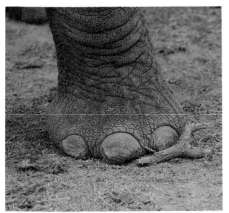

For an animal of its size and weight, the elephant has an amazingly quiet and light-footed walk. Its big feet are almost round, and the soles are tough and spongy. This bouncy quality takes the burden of weight off the elephant's leg bones.

The elephant walks at a speed of about three miles per hour. When pursued, or when

attacking, it can reach a speed of about eighteen miles per hour.

Surprisingly, elephants are very good swimmers. They can swim along underwater, holding their trunks up, using them like snorkels.

When on the move, elephants often walk in close formation.

◇ The Senses of the Elephant

Elephants depend a great deal on their good sense of smell and their excellent hearing. If they suspect danger, they stand together with their trunks held high, smelling the wind, and their ears spread out, listening. When out of each other's sight, they keep in contact with one another by using their sense of smell and by making low rumbling sounds.

Elephants have a good sense of balance. They can go up and

down very steep mountain paths and not lose their footing. On such a path, a rider would be more secure on an elephant than on a horse.

Their sense of touch is also important. Elephants use their trunks to test out unfamiliar ground before stepping on it and to feel their small calves, who walk next to them or between their legs.

Elephant skin is thick (one inch) but sensitive. Elephants powder it with dust, cool it with mud, and bathe every day if possible. In hot weather, they fan themselves by flapping their ears. They are sensitive to heat.

We don't know how much elephants depend on their eyesight. Their eyes are small and face down and to the side. But we do know that elephants are highly intelligent.

◇ How Elephants Communicate

Like many other animals, including people, elephants communicate a good deal through body language. The position of the head, the trunk, and the ears all mean something. If a dominant bull holds his head high and his ears out, this is a threat, and a smaller elephant is likely to move away.

How does an elephant say hello? It puts its trunk in another elephant's mouth or ear.

When elephants meet, they often entwine their trunks and touch one another's cheeks. Elephants recognize individual

friends by sight, smell, and voice. An elephant mother will call her baby by making a low, humming rumble.

For a long time, people thought the low rumbling sound elephants made came from their stomachs. Now we know the sound is made in the throat. They greet each other with a rumble. They also make their presence known with a rumble.

Trumpeting is more of an emergency communication. Elephants trumpet when they are attacked or when they've lost contact with the rest of the herd. Males sometimes trumpet when they are fighting one another or when they are about to attack another animal.

◇ Being Born

Elephants have no special mating season, so baby elephants are born throughout the year. The mother elephant is pregnant for twenty to twenty-two months.

When a baby is about to be born, the other females surround the mother protectively. The calf passes from the mother's body and drops down to the ground. Usually, one baby is born. Twins are born only about one out of one hundred times.

The baby's skin at birth is pinkish, and has a scattering of brown hairs. The mother, along with other adult females, pulls away the birth membrane and gently helps the baby to stand up. She pulls it to her with her trunk.

The baby elephant can stand within about fifteen minutes of birth. It's just three feet tall and weighs around 250 pounds.

Only about an hour later, the herd may move on, more slowly than usual. The new member walks between its mother and another elephant, partially supported by their trunks.

When it's a day old, the calf can walk almost a mile. One two-day-old baby elephant was seen to have walked seven miles! On day three, the herd resumes its normal walking rate. The baby can now keep up with the others.

For four or five months, the baby uses its mouth to drink its mother's milk.

◇ Growing Up

The young elephant is a clumsy little thing. It doesn't seem to know what to do with its trunk. Sometimes it steps on it. Sometimes it sucks it, the way a human baby will suck its thumb. For a few months, the young elephant never goes more than fifteen or twenty feet from its mother.

Adult elephants suck water up into their trunks, then spray it into their mouths. Young elephants don't know how to do this. So they kneel down and drink directly with their mouths.

Like all youngsters, young elephants like to play. They have make-believe fights, swinging their trunks and rushing at each other. They chase egrets and rabbits and pelicans.

Young elephants love the water. They learn to swim very

early. When crossing a river, they swim on the upstream side of the mother or another elephant.

At first young elephants live mostly on their mother's milk. After three or four months they start eating grass, leaves, and fruit as well. At first they're clumsy at this and have trouble using their trunks to bring food up to their mouths.

Young elephants are watched over by the whole herd. They have much to learn: what plants are good to eat, where the water is, where the paths are. They learn how to communicate. And they have to learn what to be afraid of, too. If a mother elephant should die, the baby may be adopted and fed by another female—but this is rare.

A female may give birth to her own first young as early as age thirteen.

◇ Living Day to Day

About four o'clock in the morning, a herd of elephants wakes up. They graze for a while, but soon they are on the move, walking close behind their leader. The herd had spent the night at the foot of a big snow-topped mountain. They get going early because they don't like to be active during the hot part of the day.

Two of the elephants in this herd of cows and calves are very young. One is about two; another is no more than a month old. They walk quietly on their padded feet, their big, dark shadows moving in the faint light of dawn. They are heading toward a certain water hole.

Where the ground is uneven, the mothers steady the little ones with their trunks. They reach the water hole at sunrise.

It's a busy place. There is a herd of zebras and a group of little wart-hogs. There are giraffes, bending to drink on their stiltlike legs. And there are a lot of other elephants.

The young elephants are happy to get into the water. They stay close to their mothers. All the elephants drink, spray themselves, and wallow in the mud. Mud helps to protect their skin.

The water hole is full now. But in the dry season, the stream that feeds it sometimes dries up. When this happens, elephants use their tusks to dig deep holes to reach underground water. Then, other animals that can't dig can use this water supply as well. They might die of thirst otherwise.

In midmorning the elephants rest near some flowering acacia trees. The big ones doze standing up, their eyes half

closed, their big ears flapping slowly. The little ones sleep on the ground, then play. After a while, the herd moves on. Through the afternoon they walk, rest, eat, and drink.

Elephants spend about sixteen hours per day eating about 300 pounds of food. Mostly they eat grass. They also pull the bark off trees. Sometimes they even knock down trees to get at the high leaves. They eat fruit when they can find it—figs, raspberries, and plums.

At dusk, the leader suddenly raises her trunk to sniff the wind. She smells danger. The others crowd behind her, the little ones under or near their mothers.

Sure enough, there are three lions in the tall grass. The elephants, even the little ones, trumpet and shake their heads. The lions slink off.

Elephants can live as long as sixty-five years. They get six sets of teeth during their lives. Elephant teeth are huge. One tooth weighs eight pounds and is about one foot long. There is only one tooth in each jaw at a time. When a tooth becomes worn down, it is pushed out and replaced by a new tooth that has been forming in the back of each jaw. When the last set wears out, old elephants can no longer chew properly. They get weaker and weaker until they die.

Elephants watch out for each other. If one is wounded or sick, two companions will walk on either side to support it and help it walk. Elephants don't like to leave a dying companion. They will gather around and try to help it. They have been seen trying to raise a dying elephant up and stuff food in its mouth. When it finally dies, they may heap vegetation on the body. Even then, they seem reluctant to leave it. But soon, of course, they must.

At about midnight, the herd stops for the night. They have walked about ten miles during the day. Under a giant baobab tree, they sleep deeply. This time, even the big ones lie down. Some of them snore. In a few hours, they will be off again, to begin a new day.

◇ Elephants in Captivity

For more than 5,000 years, Asiatic elephants have been caught and trained to do work. They can lift huge logs and carry 800-pound loads. Work elephants are trained by a person called a *mahout*. They learn to obey commands such as "Lift the log" and "Pull the chain!" African elephants have also been trained to pull wagons and carry heavy loads. Usually there is quite a lot of cruelty involved in the initial training.

Since elephants are such majestic animals, they have long been used in parades, ceremonies, and circuses. Big and strong, they were used in war by Hannibal in ancient Carthage and by Julius Caesar in ancient Rome.

Captive elephants need a lot of special care. Those at the best zoos (for example, the San Diego Wild Animal Park) are rubbed down with mineral oil and lanolin to keep their skin from getting cracked and dry. They even need to get their toenails trimmed, because they don't walk enough for the nails to wear down, as they would in the wild.

Zoo elephants eat a lot, though not as much as elephants in the wild. They are fed alfalfa, hay, cabbages, apples, carrots, beets, and potatoes. They also need a lot of water. In a year, one elephant drinks more than 15,000 gallons of water.

◇ Protecting the Elephant

In the 1930s, there were about ten million elephants in Africa. In 1979 there were about one and one-third million. By 1989, the number had dropped to only about 625,000. In other words, in the last ten years, half of the African elephants have died or been killed! Across Africa there are 360 wildlife reserves covering 430,000 square miles where animals are meant to be safe from hunters. Why is the elephant population dropping so fast?

One reason is that there is less and less wild area for all animals. Their habitat is shrinking. But in the case of elephants the main problem is poaching—the illegal killing of elephants to get their tusks for ivory. The price of ivory is now more than $150 per pound. A pair of big tusks can weight more than 400 pounds.

In 1989 a new organization, the African Elephant Co-ordinating Group, was formed in London. Included in the group are twenty-one countries and wildlife organizations. The new group is raising money to help African nations hire more rangers and provide needed equipment, like jeeps, to patrol the wildlife reserves. They also hope to involve local people in trying to prevent poaching. Wildlife preservation is costly in manpower, land, and equipment. But wildlife is precious to all of us. It is only right that we all contribute toward trying to help animals survive. In June 1989, to help prevent poaching, the United States and twelve European countries banned the import of ivory. There may soon be a total ban on the ivory trade worldwide.

The Asiatic elephant is more endangered than the African. Its total population is only about 40,000. In this case, the problem is not ivory poaching. In Sri Lanka, among the 2,500 Ceylon elephants, only 105 of the bulls have tusks. The problem is space. Most land has already been cleared for farming and

tea plantations. The remaining elephants have been squeezed into pockets of forests. The subspecies called the Malayan elephant has only 750 remaining individuals. We will have to work fast if these elephants are going to be saved from extinction.

To most of us, elephants are very special. It is our responsibility to make sure that they continue to survive—not just in zoos, but in their natural habitat, living a true elephant life in the wild.

About the Contributors

JANE GOODALL was born in London on April 3, 1934, and grew up in Bournemouth, on the southern coast of England. In 1960, she began studying chimpanzees in the wild in Gombe, Tanzania. After receiving her doctorate in ethology at Cambridge University, Dr. Goodall founded the Gombe Stream Research Center for the study of chimpanzees and baboons. In 1977, she established the Jane Goodall Institute for Wildlife Research, Education and Conservation to promote animal research throughout the world. She has written three books for adults, including the bestseller *In the Shadow of Man*, and three books for children, including the acclaimed *My Life With the Chimpanzees* and *The Chimpanzee Family Book*.

MIRIAM SCHLEIN is the author of more than sixty books for children. Six of those have been chosen as Junior Literary Guild selections, six others were named as Outstanding Science Books for Children, as selected by the National Science Teachers Association/Children's Book Council Joint Committee. She is the recipient of the Boys Clubs of America Junior Book Medal, and her book *Project Panda Watch* was cited as an Honor Book by the New York Academy of Sciences. She is also the author of *Pandas*, *Hippos*, and *Gorillas* in the Jane Goodall's Animal World series. She is the mother of two grown children and lives in New York City.

Jane Goodall's commitment to the animal world is expressed in her words, "Only when we understand can we care. Only when we care can we help. Only when we help shall they be saved." You can learn more about joining in her efforts to protect endangered wildlife by contacting The Jane Goodall Institute for Wildlife Research, Education and Conservation, P.O. Box 26846, Tucson, Arizona 85726.

Aladdin Books
Macmillan Publishing Company
866 Third Avenue, New York, NY 10022
Collier Macmillan Canada, Inc.

First Aladdin Books edition 1990

Printed in the United States of America

Cover photo copyright © by Leonard Lee Rue III
Back cover photo copyright © by Leonard Lee Rue III
Front cover photo insert of Jane Goodall by Hugo Van Lawick copyright © National Geographic Society
Introduction photo of Jane Goodall copyright © Ben Asen
Interior illustrations copyright © 1990 by Byron Preiss Visual Publications, Inc.

Interior photos copyright © Leonard Lee Rue III and Len Rue, Jr., except for the following: page 5 (bottom): copyright © David Waters/Envision; page 28: copyright © Tim Gibson/Envision; page 29 copyright © Dwight Ellefsen/Envision.

Interior illustrations by Ralph Reese

A hardcover edition of *Jane Goodall's Animal World: Elephants* is available from Atheneum Publishers, Macmillan Publishing Company.

10 9 8 7 6 5 4 3 2 1

Special thanks to Cynthia Moss, Judy Wilson, Jonathan Lanman, and Ana Cerro.

Editor: Ruth Ashby
Associate Editor: Gillian Bucky
Cover design: Ted Mader & Associates
Interior design: Alex Jay/Studio J

Library of Congress Cataloging-in-Publication Data
Schlein, Miriam.
    Jane Goodall's animal world. Elephants/by Miriam Schlein.
    —1st Aladdin Books ed.   p.   cm.
    "A Byron Preiss Book."
    Summary: An introduction to elephants, majestic, intelligent residents of Africa and Asia.
    ISBN 0-689-71395-9
    1. African elephant —Juvenile literature. [1. Elephants.] I. Title.
QL737.P98S35 1990b 599.6'1 — dc20   89-78128